Merry Christmas
Gingy + Frank!
♡ Kate + Luke

Alaska's
Watchable
Whales

Publisher and Project Editor: Mark Kelley
Photographers: Mark Kelley and John Hyde
Book and Cover Design: Laura Lucas
Writer: Linda Daniel
Foreword: Lynn Schooler
Whale Tale Interviewer: Scott Foster
Text Editor: Larry Persily
Researcher: Lena Darnall
Proofreader: Paula Cadiente
Scientific Proofreaders: Dena Matkin and Jan Straley
Printers: Samwha Printers Co., Seoul, Korea

Single copies of *Alaska's Watchable Whales* can be purchased for $14.95 plus
$5.00 for shipping and handling. Retail discounts are available for stores.

Mark Kelley can be reached at P.O. Box 20470, Juneau, AK 99802;
by phone (toll free) at (888) 933-1993 or (907) 586-1993;
by FAX at (907) 586-1201; or by e-mail at photos@markkelley.com
Website: www.markkelley.com

Printed in Korea
First Printing: March 2004
10 9 8 7 6 5 4 3 2 1

ISBN 0-9744053-0-2

Cover: A humpback whale dives in front of kayakers in Icy Strait in Southeast Alaska. Photo by Mark Kelley
Half-title page: Whale watcher glasses a humpback fluke. Photos by Mark Kelley
Title page: Humpback whales. Photo by John Hyde
Back cover: Killer whales ply the waters of Lynn Canal. Photo by Mark Kelley

Alaska's Watchable Whales

HUMPBACK & KILLER WHALES

photos by
MARK KELLEY & JOHN HYDE

Text by Linda Daniel
Whale tale interviews by Scott Foster
Foreword by Lynn Schooler

Humpback whale tails, Stephens Passage, Alaska   *photo by John Hyde*   5

Killer whale breaching, Lynn Canal   *photos by Mark Kelley*

FOREWORD
by LYNN SCHOOLER

No one — absolutely no one — stands silent and empty at their first glimpse of a whale. Ask any boat captain or naturalist who introduces visitors to Alaska's humpbacks and orcas. They all say the same thing. All have stories of seeing people brought to tears by the sight of a broad, dark back rising up from the deep.

But why does the sight of a towering killer whale fin have the power to reduce an otherwise articulate person to a vocabulary of gasps and squeaks?

Is it simply the rarity of the experience? The combined population of humans aboard two or three of the world's large cruise ships probably exceeds the total number of humpbacks on the planet.

Or is it something more ephemeral? Is it that whales' lives are full of experiences we cannot grasp? If you went swimming with a killer whale, its powers of echolocation (which operate much like a bat's radar) would allow it to "see" the beating of your heart. And no one fully

understands the purpose and capability of the humpbacks' eerie song.

Humpbacks and orcas are some of the most studied animals in the world, but beyond basic facts almost everything about them remains a mystery.

For years the evolution of whales was a mystery locked in the sediments of long-dead seas that are now parts of the deserts of Egypt and Pakistan. It wasn't until the late 1970s, when American

photo by Mark Kelley

palaeontologist Philip Gingerich found the skull of a 50-million-year-old whale in the desert of Pakistan and named it pakicetus, that there was a direct connection between whales and their land-bound predecessors. Pakicetus was a creature in transition, a primordial, 50-foot-long beast that was neither fully terrestrial nor aquatic. It had the long, lower jaw of a modern whale but the hefty, triangular molars of a very weird, now-extinct group of carnivores called mesonychids —

think meat-eating cows — that emerged 60 million years ago, shortly after the dinosaurs disappeared.

Until a century or so ago, most scientists did not even classify the air-breathing, milk-producing whales as mammals, referring to them instead as "great fish." Their confusion is understandable. Giorgio Pilleri, of the University of Berne in Switzerland, who has written extensively about the origins of whales, acknowledged:

"Nothing less resembles a mammal than a whale."

With fore limbs morphed into flippers, no hind limbs and nostrils on the top of their heads, it is hard to believe that whales are in any way related to dogs, buffalos, lemurs or humans. But our fascination with the immense creatures is compounded not only by our differences, but by behaviors and traits resembling our own.

photo by John Hyde

Whales, like humans, live in family groups, communicate with each other, and try to aid one another in distress. When a Juneau-Douglas High School science teacher discovered in the late 1970s how humpback whales use a hunting technique called bubble-net feeding to prey on schools of herring, we realized they are capable of engaging in coordinated, cooperative communal efforts.

But it has only been in the past 30 years that these and dozens of other fascinating insights into whales' lives have come to light.

In the first century A.D., Pliny the Elder described the killer whale as "a mass of flesh armed with savage teeth," and until recently the larger whales were seldom appreciated for anything more than their oil.

Fortunately, no other order of animals in history has undergone such a radical change in public perception, and now bumper stickers proclaiming "Free Willy!" and "Save the Whales!" are common.

So what's next? Will we find that some species of whales have the ability to communicate with each other across vast distances using low-frequency sound, as has recently been proved of elephants? Or that some whales cooperate with other species such as sea lions or seabirds to hunt more efficiently?

One thing is certain: There are indeed many wondrous things to learn.

Lynn Schooler is a long-time Alaskan, sailor, charter captain, guide, photographer and author of The Blue Bear.

Mark Kelley

humpback whales

killer or orca whales

Mark Kelley

whale tales — true life adventures from Alaska whale waters

Rod Judy p.21   John Hyde p.26   Steve Berry p.36   Jan Straley p.41
Sandy Craig p.44   Michael Opp p.55   Dena Matkin p.58   Jim Collins p.67

humpback whales

Megaptera novaeangliae

A veil of mist from the humpback's exhale showers an enormous hump.
photo by Mark Kelley

The humpback's name

The humpback's name comes from the rounded hump people see as it dives. Pointing its head toward the bottom, the whale rolls forward and lifts its tail or flukes. What looks like a hump is 49 feet of back rolling into a headstand and plunging 60,000 pounds into a downward voyage.

Mammalian traits

Most people know whales are not fish, but mammals that give live birth and nurse their young. Like all mammals they breathe air, coming to the surface to exhale and inhale. What's news to many is that humpbacks have another mammalian trait: they grow hair. It sprouts from bumps called tubercles on their chins and above their jaws. No one knows why the hair is there, though some scientists speculate it may serve as feelers, much like a cat's whiskers.

(right)
Barnacles cling to the surface of the whale's pleated chin below its tubercles.
photo by Mark Kelley

photo by John Hyde

Age and size

Lack of teeth doesn't bother a whale, but it poses a problem for researchers. Biologists normally look at the teeth to determine a mammal's age. Marine biologists estimate the age of dead baleen whales by looking at the ear plug, a waxy substance laid down annually. Biologists count the years of growth like the rings of a tree. During commercial whaling days, the oldest humpback killed was 48 years old.

Humpbacks grow to lengths of 42 to 49 feet. Like all baleen whales, females are slightly larger than males, which weigh about 25 tons to the females' 35 tons. The humpback is the sixth largest whale in the world. The blue whale is largest, with the fin, sperm, bowhead, right and humpback whales following in order. Interestingly, measurements of whales taken during commercial whaling indicated that southern hemisphere humpbacks grew larger than those in the northern hemisphere.

Humpbacks are black or dark gray with some white on the throat, flukes, and the wing-like flippers called pectoral fins.

Range and migration

Humpbacks are long-distance ocean travelers and migrate each year between their winter birth-places in the tropics and the Alaska feeding grounds where their mothers brought them as calves. No one knows how they find their way to the same place year after year. Some researchers think the whales use the stars or sun to navigate, checking land-marks as they leap out of the water or spyhop. Others believe iron deposits in the frontal lobe of their brain allow whales to read the earth's magnetic field like a map.

Most humpbacks that feed in Southeast Alaska and Prince William Sound migrate to Hawaii in fall or early winter. Other Pacific humpbacks winter near Mexico or Japan.

A few North Pacific humpbacks have been sighted off Costa Rica.

The speed record for migration between Southeast Alaska and Hawaii belongs to a whale that made the nearly 3,000-mile run in 36 days, averaging about 83 miles a day. Humpbacks normally swim at 3 to 9 miles per hour, with an average about 5 miles per hour, and can accelerate for short bursts of speed.

photo by Mark Kelley

19

photo by Mark Kelley

whale tales

as told by
Rod Judy

"I FLEW IN MY FLOATPLANE to pick up some Forest Service guys who were putting out a small fire on the Keku Islands near Kake.

"It took about 15 minutes to load all the stuff, and during that time we never heard a whale. Usually, you know, you hear one blow or do something. We had no idea one was there. And the water was relatively shallow. Well, after we loaded up we taxied off.

"Just about the time we lifted off the water, this whale breached right in front of us. I saw this whale's stomach. You could see all the little ridges on its stomach and I saw what looked like a big old black eye. We were probably eight or 10 feet above the water.

"I didn't have time to think. I probably just let my foot off the rudder pedal and the airplane turned by itself, mainly because I was startled. The airplane went left, and it's a good thing the whale went to our right.

"I thought we were within 100 feet of the whale. My passenger thought we were 10 feet. I think it was more exciting for the passenger than it was for me. He sputtered and spit. He could hardly talk all the way back.

"He's the one who told the story to The Associated Press. He was saying, 'In another second we would have been a necklace around the whale's neck.'

"I heard from people all over the country after the AP did the story. Every time I talked to somebody, they'd mention it. And it was on Paul Harvey."

Rod Judy is a pilot and owner of Pacific Wings *in Petersburg, Alaska.*

photo by Mark Kelley

photo by Mark Kelley

Baleen or toothless whales

The whale that swallowed Jonah certainly wasn't a humpback. A man would stick in a humpback's throat, so small that nothing bigger than a grapefruit will go down. Because they have no teeth, humpbacks eat only what is small enough to swallow whole. In Alaska waters, humpbacks savor zooplankton, a shrimp-like crustacean called krill, and herring-size fish.

The humpback belongs to a sub-order of whales called baleen or toothless whales. They eat by taking a mouthful of prey-laden seawater, spewing out the water, and gulping down what's left. Their mouths are equipped with strainers that look like rows of fine-toothed combs hanging from each side the upper jaw in place of teeth. The strainers consist of baleen plates, up to 400 of them set

side by side. Each plate is solid at the base and frays out into fine hairs up to 30 inches long in the middle of the mouth. The baleen is shorter at the front and back of the mouth. These strong, flexible baleen hairs were the "whalebone" that stiffened ladies' corsets a century ago.

Alaska's cold water combines with long hours of summer daylight to produce a sea rich in prey. Humpbacks eat almost constantly, consuming over a third of a ton of food a day. They are catching up for the meals they skipped in the past three to four months during migration and while on the tropical wintering grounds, where they eat little or nothing at all.

The humpback has a double chin, but not from all that eating. The chin expands like an accordion. Pleats run down the lower jaw from the tip of the chin to the belly. When the whale opens wide, the lower jaw drops more than 90 degrees and the chin balloons out. The result is a cavernous mouth that can hold 15,000 gallons of seawater teeming with prey. Imagine a mouthful of seven Volkswagen Beetles awash in 160,000 cans of soda pop.

Bubbles from the humpbacks' bubble-net surround the surfacing whales.
photos by Mark Kelley

Lunge feeding and bubble-netting

Humpbacks use two special feeding techniques, lunge and bubble-net feeding. A whale lunging upward with mouth wide open can scoop up a small school of fish or krill. Whales lunge feed alone or in groups, synchronizing their lunging and diving, and using an occasional tail flick to herd their prey.

Bubble-net feeding can be a team effort involving up to two dozen whales. They dive below a school of fish, swim into a circle, and start blowing a ring of bubbles. As the bubbles rise, they form a curtain around a column of water. The fish stay within the encircling bubbles as if trapped in a net. The whales then swim up from under the fish, with their mouths wide open, engulfing the concentrated prey. Single whales can use smaller bubble nets to capture swarms of krill at the surface.

written by
John Hyde

I WAS PHOTOGRAPHING humpback whales from my 14-foot inflatable off Admiralty Island's northern peninsula. The hydrophone dangling over the side had enabled me to listen to the whale's feeding calls. The louder they were, the closer they were. When the calls stopped, I knew the herring would break the surface within seconds, followed by gaping jaws hung with baleen and huge pink tongues.

Even from my low vantage point in the raft, I could see rising bubbles as they betrayed the location of the bubble nets the whales were using to confine their prey. The gulls were circling above, watching for bubbles as well. With their high vantage point, they could see them well before I could. When the gulls broke formation and streaked down, I knew that was where the whales were going to surface.

Meanwhile, a young girl aboard a boat a few hundred feet away was shooting a video of the scene. She asked her dad, "Where are the whales going to come up?" Her father replied, "Just watch the guy in the little red boat. They'll come up wherever he points that big white lens."

If the whales followed their foraging pattern they would be going down again, and I had time to start lunch. I popped the lid on my cooler and reached for a sandwich and a can of iced tea. I'd eaten a few bites when I saw a few small bubbles off the side of the boat. The wind had come up and tiny whitecaps were forming in the ripples of the current line, so I didn't think too much of it.

A few seconds later a large bubble about the size of a basketball broke the surface. Followed by another and another, they began to form an arc around my small boat. Sitting smack in the middle of a huge bubble net with as many as two dozen humpback whales coming in my direction as fast as they could didn't offer many options for escape. I had lots of pictures from the day and valued the safety of my equipment and, yes, even my life. So, the cameras went into the cooler while I figured staying put was the safest thing to do.

Almost as soon as I'd gotten on top of the cooler the whales completed their lunge. Rising up all around me, they jostled my tiny craft from all sides. Wet, black shiny skin seemed to envelope me as water sloshed into the boat and herring fell from the sky. As I frantically spun around trying to determine my fate, glimpses of tails, towering pectoral fins, baleen, barnacles and sea lice were punctuated with the explosive blows of huge mammals filling lungs the size of Volkswagens.

Bit by bit more space opened up around the boat as things began to settle down — all except my pulse rate.

Within 30 seconds the whales were on their way, leaving me to contemplate my amazing good fortune to still be afloat and alive. In a kind of daze, I began to pluck a dozen of so herring off the floor of the boat, tossing them back to the sea.

The videographers came over to check on me and to offer me a copy of the video, which I gladly accepted, silently vowing never to show my mother.

John Hyde is a wildlife photographer whose photos are featured in this book.

photo by John Hyde

Watchable behaviors

Humpbacks, with their wing-like pectoral fins, are the most acrobatic and showy of all whales. They wave and slap their fins against the water, leap clear out of it, or dive with their flukes silhouetted against the sky when making a long, deep dive called a sounding.

Part of the humpback's appeal is its repertoire of routines that are anything but routine to first-time sightseers — or even to the most experienced researcher. Scientists speculate at the meaning and purpose of some of the whale's behavior, and no one knows for sure why the whales slap their fins and tails on the surface or go spyhopping.

photo by John Hyde

photo by John Hyde

Breaching

Humpback's breaching behavior leaves researchers scratching their heads for a definitive answer. Why do the whales leap completely out of the water? It could be to wash barnacles from their skin, to see into the distance, to communicate with other whales, or just to play. A humpback once was seen breaching more than 40 times in succession. Whales often start breaching when the weather changes in response to a drop in barometric pressure. When the wind picks up and the seas get choppy, they typically breach into the wind and land on their backs to protect their bellies.

Blows

Vaporous evidence of a whale's presence, the spout of a humpback is frequently the first sign a whalewatcher spots.

Each humpback has a paired blowhole, the equivalent of nostrils atop its head. They emit a spray 6 to 10 feet high as the whale exchanges 80 percent of the air from its car-sized lungs. The mist hangs in the air long after the whale has submerged.

photo by John Hyde

photo by John Hyde

31

Spyhopping

Just as a submarine raises its periscope to look around, humpbacks take an occasional peek above sea level. A humpback spyhops when it lifts the top third of its body (just past the eyes) out of the water. The whale may shoot up 10 to 12 feet, sometimes spinning around to get a good look before sliding gracefully back into the water. Some researchers think this helps with navigation.

photo by John Hyde

Humpback pectoral fins are usually dark on the topside and white on the underside.

photos by Mark Kelley

Pectoral fins

The humpback's scientific name, *Megaptera novaeangliae*, means "great-winged New Englander." The humpback's enormous pectoral fins — longest of all the world's whales — look like wings and are just as versatile. Up to 15 feet long or about one-third of the whale's total length, they act as a cooling system. Blood vessels run through the fin just beneath the skin and close to the water. The water chills the blood, which then runs like a coolant throughout the body.

Fin or flipper slapping

Humpbacks may also use their pectoral fins to communicate by flipper slapping, producing a smack sounding like a gunshot that can be heard for miles. Sometimes the flippers are used to herd prey forward toward the whale's mouth. During mating season, competing males use their flippers as weapons as they ram each other. The flippers are formidable weapons, strong from swimming and sharp with barnacles.

Tail or flukes

The humpback's powerful tail, called flukes, is set crosswise to the body, like an airplane's wing. The flukes measure up to 15 feet from tip to tip. The tail moves up and down rather than fishtailing sideways.

The shape of the flukes and the black-and-white markings on the underside are unique to each whale, much like a human fingerprint. Researchers use these markings to tell one whale from another, allowing them to track an individual whale over time.

Tail lobbing

A humpback may repeatedly slap its flukes against the water, a practice called tail lobbing.

photo by John Hyde

photo by Mark Kelley

Dive or sounding

At a distance, it's easy to confuse a humpback with the other big whales because their dorsal fins and blows look much alike. But only the humpback consistently lifts its flukes skyward when making a deep dive. Humpbacks stay under an average of five to eight minutes in Alaska, with some very long dives lasting up to 20 minutes. These long dives make it hard to know where to look for the whale to reappear.

The longest recorded sounding was 45 minutes in the tropical waters of Hawaii. The deepest measured dive of any humpback was just short of 600 feet.

as told by
Steve Berry ·

"I CAN TELL YOU EXACTLY when it happened. July 2, 1995. 6:10 p.m. It's ever ingrained in my memory. We were whale watching off North Kupreanof Island. The engines were stopped.

"This one whale that I'd seen over and over, the way it would dive, I knew it was going to breach…I told the people, 'This one's going to breach!'

"We waited and waited and waited and sure enough it breached right off the bow. You know how they kind of do a pirouette and spin around. And as it spun around its pectoral fin came right down on the bow of the boat. Just about flipped (our 28-foot) boat over!

"I had three people standing exactly where its pectoral fin hit. I don't know how anybody didn't get hurt. They went into the water…we were able to get the people out of the water. They were OK.

"Of course the whale slipped off. And the boat bounced up. I hung on and two other passengers held on.

"When I got everyone out of the water we all started asking, 'What happened?' 'How did it happen?' 'Where did the whale go?' 'How is the whale?'

"The whale swam off. It probably had a sore pec.

"At that time, that was the only known documentation of a whale ever breaching and landing on a boat in the United States. Since then a whale breached and landed on a boat in which the captain was killed. That was down in Moro Bay, California.

"I've fished in the Bering Sea and fished out of Petersburg for 20 years before I started my charter business. And without a doubt, without a doubt, this was the most terrifying experience I've ever had."

Steve Berry is a charter boat captain in Petersburg, Alaska.

photo by Mark Kelley

Sounds and language

Humpbacks are known as the "songsters of the sea" because of the unique, varied sounds they make. They communicate with each other through sounds ranging from low-frequency moans to high-pitched chirps. Swimmers and scuba divers can hear the vocalizations within a radius of five miles, while researchers think whales can hear each other from even farther away. Under the right conditions and sitting quietly in a boat with the engine off, a person can hear humpbacks vocalize as the sound reverberates through the boat's hull.

A hydrophone hung over the side of a boat in Alaska lets people hear the whales' feeding call, or trumpet call. Comprised of 5 to 30 phrases that increase in pitch, each phrase lasts five to eight seconds during bubble-net feeding. Researchers theorize that humpbacks use the call to co-ordinate group feeding or to herd their prey to the surface.

Most of the sounds are of a very low frequency, punctuated with higher ones. Whales don't have vocal cords, and scientists really do not know how baleen whales produce sound. The current theory is that these sounds are produced by a combination of the larynx and the resonant qualities of the bony nasal passage. Like a good ventriloquist, the whale's mouth doesn't move and no air escapes during vocalizing.

Birth, babies and adolescence

Calves are born in warm waters because they have little or no blubber at birth. Without that insulating layer, calves would not survive in the cold Alaska seas. While in Hawaii and during migration, the nursing calves build up fat by consuming gallons of milk a day. Up to 50 percent milk fat, whales' milk is one of the richest on earth. A newborn calf weighs about two tons and is approximately 14 feet long. It grows quickly while nursing on its mother's rich milk. Calves start to eat on their own when they are about six months old, weighing 10 tons. About 80 percent of calves survive their first migration to the feeding grounds. Most leave their mothers before the south-bound migration in the fall or early winter.

While mother and calf are together, the mother is very nurturing. She holds and caresses her calf with her long pectoral fins and may cruise on the surface with an infant riding on top of her head. Humpbacks fervently protect their calves. When a calf is threatened, other whales will join the mother to protect the calf.

The 11- to 12-month gestation period synchronizes perfectly with the whales' migration. The mother gives birth to a single calf on south-bound migration or soon after arriving on the tropical mating and calving grounds. She will give birth once every two or three years for the rest of her life.

In the North Pacific, the youngest humpback known to give birth was eight years old.

A juvenile humpback less than 12 months old clears the surface of the water in a full breach.
photo by John Hyde

Populations and predators

Humpback whales are listed as an
endangered species in U.S. waters.
Scientists estimate there are about
8,000 whales in the North Pacific.
An estimated 1,000 humpbacks
spend their summer in northern
Southeast Alaska, with another 200
in Prince William Sound, 400
around the Shumagin Islands along
the Aleutian Chain, and 650 near
Kodiak.

There were thought to be fewer
than 1,000 humpbacks worldwide in
1966, when commercial whaling
was banned. They were easy targets
for whalers because humpbacks
swim slowly and spend most of their
time near shore. Nearly 28,000
humpbacks were killed by whalers
between 1905 and 1965, 23,000 of
them in the North Pacific alone.

photo by Mark Kelley

In the early 1970s, Congress passed both the U.S. Marine Mammal Protection Act and the Endangered Species Act, protecting the humpback population from commercial harvest and other threats. The Federal Humpback Whale Recovery Plan of 1991 focused on rebuilding humpback populations.

Although the humpback's natural enemies include killer whales, great white and tiger sharks, humans pose the greatest threat. Boats accidentally hit whales. Commercial fishers sometimes catch them in nets or the whales become tangled in pot lines or long-line gear. But, the biggest potential threat to humpbacks today is loss of habitat and food, serving as a reminder that although their population is recovering from exploitation, they are still at risk.

as told by
Jan Straley

"GLACIER BAY BIOLOGIST Christine Gabriele, the Coast Guard ship *Liberty* and I responded to a report that a humpback whale had wrapped itself around two buoy lines from shrimp pots near Skagway.

"It was December, so we knew we had a limited amount of time because of the short daylight. Fortunately the water was really calm. If it had been choppy at all, it probably would have been impossible to accomplish anything because you wouldn't have been able to see.

"We approached the whale in a small, inflatable boat to do an assessment. By using a face mask and snorkel and putting our head underwater we could see the lines were wrapped about the main part of the whale's body, forward of the pectoral fin.

"We worked on top of the whale in this little boat for two hours or so. I was driving. You really needed to know whale behavior and try to guess what the whale was going to do. The whale was just a few feet beneath us. Sometimes it was even closer when it came up to breathe.

"If the whale didn't want us there it could have thrown us into the water. It was a little unnerving, but the longer we worked, the more comfortable we got that the whale wasn't going to do anything drastic.

"We used hooked knives on a pole to get underneath the line, which was very tight. There were a lot of steps to go through to realize exactly what we needed to do and when and what to cut first.

"It was a very big relief when we got the whale free. I don't want to do that very often or at all."

Jan Straley is a marine biologist in Sitka, Alaska.

Humpback whale facts

		Average	Range
Length	Female		45-49 feet
	Male		42-46 feet
	At birth	14 feet	12-16 feet
Weight	Female	35 tons	25-40 tons
	Male	25 tons	25-30 tons
	At birth	2 tons	
Anatomy	Flukes (length)	15 feet each	
	Flipper (length)	15 feet each	1/3 overall body
	Ventral pleats	10-36 pleats	
	Baleen (per side)	400 plates	270-400 plates
Behaviors	Blow	6 feet high	Up to 10 feet
	Dive: time	About 5 minutes	2-15 minutes
	Dive: depth	120 feet	Surface to 600 feet
	Vocalizations	100-4,000 hertz	
	Whalesong: time	Males: 15 minutes	10-45 minutes
	Adult feeding habits	About 1/3 of a ton per day	Unknown
Life history	Lifespan	Estimate: human life span	
	Sexual maturity	5 years	4-6 years
	Gestation	11.5 months	
	Lactation	10 months	6-10 months
Populations	World	Unknown	
	North Pacific	About 8,000 whales	
	Southeast Alaska	About 1,000 whales	
Migration	Between Hawaii and Alaska	Fastest transit: about 1 month	
	Roundtrip Hawaii - Alaska	6,000 miles per year	

43

whale tales

as told by
Sandy Craig

"WE WERE ANCHORED in 50 feet of water at the head of Lisianski Inlet about 300 feet from shore, and it was flat calm. Then, in the middle of the night, the boat just went crashing over on its side!

"I went running from my bunk to the back deck. The water was boiling around the boat, but everything else was calm.

"I ran up to the bow. By the time I got there, the boat was doing seven or eight knots. We were headed out to sea. I couldn't figure out what was going on. It was so scary!

"Joe (my husband) yelled 'It's a whale!'

"I looked at the anchor line, and it just started coming up. And about 50 feet in front of the boat, a whale's tail goes 'Whoosh. Whoosh.'

"Joe runs up. He had a knife and asked me, because it was my anchor gear, 'Can I cut it?'

"'Yeah!' I yelled. 'As soon as possible!'

"He just touched that line with the knife and it broke.

"Then the whale came out of the water, like three times. I guess he was shaking off the anchor gear. Then he just laid on the surface and started cruising around the boat, snorting .

"We talked about Moby Dick. Joe thought the whale was angry. I thought it was relieved. In a while the whale went back to feeding.

"Eventually, we motored back to where we had anchored. Looking at my depth finder, I couldn't find the bottom because there was so much feed in the water. So I think the whale didn't see us, just came up underneath, startled itself, took off and got the anchor line tied around one of its fins.

"I think we were pulled for several minutes. It was like a Nantucket sleigh ride!"

Sandy Craig is a charter boat captain and commercial fisherman from Elfin Cove, Alaska.

photo by John Hyde

44

killer whales

Orcinus orca

Cute or killers?

It's hard to believe the endearing cetaceans introduced to audiences in the film "Free Willy" are also fierce predators that go by the name "killer." Orcas, or killer whales, are the most recognizable of the whales with their striking black-and-white coloring, a white chin and belly, and a white patch behind each eye.

Size and speed

An orca can be as long as 33 feet and weigh as much as 11 tons, but that would be one whale of a guy. The average adult male is around 26 feet long and weighs about 8 tons. The average adult female is about 3 feet shorter than the male and weighs about half as much, a petite 4 tons. Some females, however, are 28 feet long and weigh 7 tons.

Orcas are one of the fastest animals in the sea, capable of swimming at top speeds of 30 to 34 miles an hour and covering as many as 100 miles per day. Orcas usually cruise about 3.5 miles an hour, but they are capable of setting a cruising pace of up to 8 miles an hour.

Dorsal fins

The orca is the largest member of the dolphin family in the suborder of toothed whales. But even the closest of relatives look different from one and another, and whale researchers can identify individual orcas by their dorsal fins. The pattern of notches on each dorsal fin is unique. Also, some orcas have gray or white saddles behind their dorsal fins. The saddles vary in shape and size and are unique to each individual. Scratches on the saddle patch further help researchers identify individual whales.

You can also tell the sex of most orcas by looking at their dorsal fins. The fin on the female's back is no more than three feet tall. The dorsal fin of a young male looks just like a female's, but when he is full-grown the fin stands up straight and can measure six feet tall. Every orca has large, paddle-like pectoral flippers and a single, crescent-shaped blowhole.

(above) Whale researchers call this whale "Zorro", recognizing this individual by the unique pattern of notches on the dorsal fin.

(right) The tall dorsal of this whale identifies it as a male.

photos by Mark Kelley

Social structure

Orcas may be killers, but they have a stable family life. They live in groups called pods, with each pod consisting of a mother and her offspring, 3 to 40 whales in all. Large pods may break up into smaller units called subpods. A female leads each subpod, and its members travel and feed together their entire lives. A male may leave briefly to mate with a female from another group, but he always returns to the family of his birth.

Pods sometimes meet up and form a superpod, with two or more pods cruising together for a month or more. The get-togethers occur in summer and early fall when food is abundant.

Residents and transients

Pods are either resident, remaining in the same general area all year, or transient, roaming far afield. Another major difference is that residents eat fish while transients eat marine mammals such as seals. Scientists have studied the stomach contents of dead orcas washed up on beaches along the North American coast and report finding either fish or mammals, but never both in the same whale. Genetic scientists believe that resident and transient orcas have not interbred for thousands of years. Researchers rarely see them interact.

photo by John Hyde

50

Migration

In the summer, resident pods tend to stay in coastal waters within 250 miles of shore. Some resident pods may cruise 1,000 miles up and down the coast, but 500 miles is a more typical range.

By contrast, transient pods are real travelers. One group of transients was sighted in Glacier Bay and was seen a few years later along the California coast, 1,500 miles away. Other transient groups head north into the Bering Strait as the pack ice retreats in the spring.

Group dynamics

Resident pods tend to be larger than transient groups, which often consist of no more than a half-dozen whales. Resident pods are noisy, playful and sociable. When a neighboring resident pod appears, the two groups greet each other, form facing lines, and swim underwater toward each other. When they meet, they leap up and chase one another, talking all the time.

Resident pods attract other mammals. Dall's porpoises, which also are black and white, often swim with them. Observers mistake the porpoises for baby killer whales. One Dall's porpoise lived with a resident pod for an entire summer, acting like a miniature killer whale. The porpoises and other marine mammals can sense the difference between resident and transient killer whales, interacting with the residents but becoming silent or leaving the water when a transient killer whale is near. Transient groups are quieter than residents, making them harder for researchers to spot and track. That also makes them effective as predators that count on stealth or surprise when hunting.

A third type of orcas, the off-shores, stays farther out in the ocean, where they are sometimes found in groups of 60 or more. The off-shores act more like residents than transients, but do not appear to associate with either of the other pod types. Little is know about these animals because they range beyond the reach of most researchers.

(left) photo by John Hyde

Feeding

As apex predators, orcas survive at the top of the food chain. In long-ago whaling days, crewmen watched them kill whales and referred to the orcas as "killers of whales." Over time the name was shortened to killer whales. The original scientific name was *Delphinus orca*, or demon dolphin. Their present-day scientific name, *Orinus orca*, means "bringer of death." Orcas have been known to have dinner with their close relative, the dolphin, with the dolphin as the entree. Orcas also eat fish, elephant seals, sea lions, stingrays, squid, turtles, birds, and even an occasional moose — the most varied diet of all the whales.

As one might expect, the orca has a serious set of teeth. They're big, sharp, interlocking and set in pairs so the uppers and lowers fit tightly together when the whale chomps into its prey. They have

whale tales

as told by
Michael Opp

"I WAS TROLLING FOR SALMON in my 15-foot skiff near Pleasant Island Reef in Icy Strait. There was another guy in a skiff nearby.

"We noticed two brown dots on the horizon coming from Chichagof Island. As they got closer we saw it was a cow and calf moose swimming across Icy Strait which at that point is 10 miles across! I thought that was pretty amazing by itself.

"Then four killer whales showed up.

"The moose separated. The killer whales went after the cow. First we thought, let's try to save this moose. We were going to take our skiffs and try to head off the killer whales. Then we thought that probably wouldn't be smart. We didn't want to interfere with the food chain and become part of it ourselves.

"The cow moose made it to about half a mile from Pleasant Island. Then there was all this thrashing in the water. The killer whales consumed her in less than 30 seconds!

"We headed back to the reef. The calf had worked itself into the center of this kelp bed that's probably 100 yards in diameter.

"Then the killer whales came.

"They circled the reef for a while. Eventually the big male tried to work his way toward the calf. He got all tangled up with kelp hanging off his dorsal fin. He'd thrash and jump way up and throw the kelp off and try to get closer. But he couldn't. Eventually the killer whales gave up and disappeared.

"About five days later I found the calf carcass on the beach at Pleasant Island. It hadn't been eaten. Who knows what caused its death, but it didn't make it."

Michael Opp is an educational administrator in Juneau, Alaska.

40 to 52 teeth, each about three inches tall and an inch in diameter. Orcas use their teeth to catch, hold and tear apart prey. They don't chew their food, but gulp it down whole or in big chunks.

A healthy orca eats about 130 pounds a day. Researchers have found more than 22 different kinds of mammals in the transients' stomachs. However, a transient group may specialize on a particular prey such as seals or porpoises and, to a lesser extent, on sea lions and large whales. In extremely rare situations, they attack sea otters.

Residents eat many kinds of fish, including salmon, herring, halibut and cod. Even though the waters around Alaska are full of pink salmon, orcas prefer to eat silver and king salmon, which are larger and richer in oil.

Whether seeking fish or mammals, the orcas' ability to communicate with one another makes them efficient hunters. Resident pods herd schools of salmon together, form a living corral around the fish, and take turns eating.

Transients, working together, can bring down even the largest whales. A story in National Geographic described how 30 orcas attacked a 60-foot blue whale. Some concentrated on trying to cover its blowholes and keep it from surfacing, while others were gnawing on its fins and tail. Pack attacks give rise to another nickname for orcas, the "wolves of the sea." In 1997 off the Farallon Islands in California, researchers videotaped a 20-foot orca killing a great white shark.

photo by John Hyde

as told by
Dena Matkin

"THREE OF US were in a Boston Whaler, and we came upon four killer whales. We stopped to watch and then saw a seal in the water with them.

"The seal was really afraid of getting caught. It came up to our boat for protection. You could read fear in its face. Its eyes were bulging. However, the seal was so unafraid of us that it actually allowed me to touch it.

"I guess that made the seal even more unafraid of us, and it decided to get away from the killer whales by getting into the boat. It made a couple of attempts, and using its flippers finally climbed in over the back. By then I figured I'd hurt the seal by trying to get it out or starting the engine.

"We had hydrophones in the water and could hear the killer whales echolocating at the boat. So they definitely knew the seal was there.

"The killer whales dove underneath us and kind of circled around, but they stayed about a whale's length away. Females average about 25 feet in length. Our boat was 15 feet.

"If the killer whales were going to do something aggressive, that would have been the situation of all situations. They could have pushed us around, or they could have breached and splashed us or stuff like that. They just let us be. I think of the word, polite. They really were. My fear of killer whales just completely went away after that experience.

"Eventually, one of my passengers needed to get back to shore. A nearby boat came to pick him up, and the whales dispersed. Then the seal, who had been in the boat for about 20 minutes, jumped out. So we probably did save its life."

Dena Matkin is a marine biologist living in Gustavus, Alaska.

Orcas sometimes stun their prey by swatting or throwing the quarry into the air with their flukes or head. They even jump out of the water to snatch seals and sea lions from rocks and beaches. In Antarctica, two orcas were seen tipping an iceberg so that a sleeping seal slid into the jaws of a waiting killer whale.

In Alaska, a harbor seal fleeing from orcas jumped aboard and hid on a researcher's boat while the whales spyhopped, called loudly and approached the 15-foot Boston Whaler before finally giving up.

The whale's diet does not include humans. However, an orca once grabbed and then quickly released a surfer, possibly mistaking the man and his surfboard for a marine mammal with a similar shape.

photo by Mark Kelley

photo by Mark Kelley

Breathing

The first thing whale watchers are likely to see isn't an orca itself, but a bushy mist of water vapor up to 10 feet high as the whale vents spent air. When orcas come up to breathe, they usually take several breaths in a row with a shallow dive after each. They then take a longer dive before disappearing. The short dives last about 30 seconds, while the longer ones are 4 to 10 minutes apart. Orcas can stay underwater for 20 minutes and dive more than 800 feet.

photo by Mark Kelley

Sleeping

Whales do not breathe automatically, without moving, as humans do. The whole pod dozes together in one big slumber party, breathing in unison while swimming slowly and making shallow dives.

Logging

When a group of orcas lies side by side on the surface like a raft of logs, it is called logging. This lazy activity involves lying motionless, facing the same direction. Logging whales are not sleeping, just hanging out together, resting and talking.

Fin slapping

Sporadically slapping flukes or flippers against the water may be a form of communication, a fish-herding technique or a means of stunning fish to make them easier to catch.

Spyhopping

A spyhopping orca lifts the upper third of its body just high enough so that the head and eyeballs clear the water. The hop lets the animal take a look around, checking the area or watching for other whales or signs of prey. Orcas have sharp eyes and can see equally well underwater or above.

Tail lobbing

When an orca slaps its tail on the surface, it's called tail lobbing. The behavior could be a warning directed at anything the orca believes is threatening or a multi-purpose communication tool. The whales use their powerful tails as weapons against their prey.

photos by John Hyde

photo by John Hyde

Breaching

Spectacular leaps above the water, called breaching, are not uncommon. These leaps, which end in a big splash, may be meant to startle prey, to communicate, or simply to play. The whales breach more often when they are courting, sometimes leaping 30 feet.

Rubbing

It appears orcas like good massages. They enjoy rubbing up against kelp and may spend hours in a kelp bed, resting and playing. They also swim into shallow water and rub their bodies against the bottom. For this activity, called beach rubbing, they choose a place where the bottom slopes sharply and is covered with small, round pebbles. In Alaska, whale watchers sometimes see orcas beach rubbing in Prince William Sound.

(left) photo by Mark Kelley

Sounds and language

Orcas vocalize a lot, and some might even call it singing. When musician Paul Winter serenaded a pod, the orcas sang back in a recorded duet. Humans can hear these most vocal of whales with the unaided ear or through a hydrophone hung in the water. Researchers have identified 62 different clicks, whistles and calls that orcas make.

Like all toothed whales, orcas vocalize to help them "see" under-water. The sound waves bounce off objects and come back as echoes. This technique, called echolocation, helps the whales find food and navigate. For echolocation, orcas use high-energy clicks, sending out several hundred clicks in a burst.

An orca rotates sideways underwater.
photo by Mark Kelley

Besides the clicks, orcas make other sounds to communicate, primarily shrill whistles and high-pitched calls. They "talk" most when there is a lot going on. The orca's language doesn't change much with the passage of time. In fact, a study of one pod's language over 30 years found that it did not change at all.

Resident pods usually vocalize more than transients do. The residents use up to 15 distinct calls. Transient groups use the language more sparingly, and have only four to seven calls. Each family group has its own unique and recognizable sounds.

as told by
Jim Collins

"I'VE SPENT 16 YEARS WORKING on the water with whales, everyday. Once, in Lynn Canal, I saw this pod of 20 to 30 killer whales. They're very much a social and very gregarious pod.

"I turned the motor off. Eventually, about four or five came over to this little boat I was in. Two of them were juvenile males. They stayed there, and seemed to play around a little.

"Then at one point, they caught a salmon and brought it over to the boat. This is a distance of 10 to 12 feet. They brought it over, opened their mouth and released the salmon. The salmon had been squeezed pretty hard so it was just on the surface twitching.

"I sat there looking at them and thought, 'I don't know what you guys want me to do but I'm not going to grab that salmon because that's yours.'

"It was a glassy calm, sunny day with great visibility. They were at a stop at the surface. We could easily see each other's eyes. Oh, yeah, they were looking at me.

"They drifted off a little, and I drifted a little away from the salmon. So they came back in, grabbed the salmon and brought it back to the boat again…the same thing. Open the mouth. Release the salmon.

"Once again I didn't grab the salmon. I just watched. Then they came in and ripped the salmon in half, and brought me the two halves. But I still didn't want to grab it.

"After that they came back, ate the salmon and left.

"I couldn't begin to tell you what was happening. The best I can say is that there was some sort of interaction going on there, and I just wasn't smart enough to figure out what it was."

Jim Collins guides whale watching excursions for Allen Marine Tours in Juneau, Alaska.

Birth, babies and adolescence

Considering how sociable orcas are,
it should come as no surprise that
mothers and calves are rarely more
than a few body lengths apart or that
it takes a pod to raise a calf. Every
member helps teach the calf to hunt
and survive. Helpful older sisters,
often stay within a few hundred yards
of a calf and its mother. Those sisters
have a fairly long wait before bearing
babies of their own.

Young orcas usually reach adulthood in the pre- and early teens, females at 10 to 15 and males at 12 to 14 years. Size more than age signals adulthood. When an orca reaches 14 to 17 feet in length, it is considered an adult. The adolescent male's dorsal fin sprouts much taller than the female's, signaling his sexual maturity. Although adulthood takes a while, orcas live a long time compared with most animals in the wild. Females have an average lifespan of 50 to 60 years, with the males getting the shorter end of the chart and sometimes living only half of that.

Mating season stretches from December to June in the southern hemisphere and from July to September in the north. Orcas mate belly to belly underwater and give birth year-round after a 17-month pregnancy. In the North Pacific, more calves are born between fall and spring than in other months of the year.

A female orca gives birth to one calf at a time, and can bear a calf every 3 to 10 years until she is about 40 years old. Born tail first, the baby orca will measure between 7 and 8 feet long and weigh about 400 pounds. Though it begins swimming immediately, it needs its mother and often a sister to help it to the surface for its first breath.

Orcas don't have lips, so the calf can't nurse as do kittens and puppies. The mother orca contracts her mammary gland to squirt a jet of hot, fatty milk into the calf's mouth. She will continue to feed her calf for about 16 months. By that time, the youngster will be about 10 feet long.

photo by Mark Kelley

photo by Mark Kelley

Population and predators

Orcas have relatives all over the world, except where polar ice keeps them from surfacing to breathe. They don't seem to mind if the climate is warm or cold, and they thrive in estuaries, where freshwater rivers mix with saltwater, as well as on the high seas.

Alaska, from the western Alaska Peninsula to the Southeast Alaska panhandle, is home to about 1,500 orcas, both resident and transients. The worldwide population of killer whales is unknown, but the species is abundant and in no danger of extinction, with humans being the orca's only known predator.

In the past, orcas were killed for their meat and oil. The next threat came from commercial fishermen, who killed orcas that were stealing fish caught in their lines and nets. Now it is illegal to kill an orca. The Marine Mammal Protection Act of 1972 reduced the human threat by

photo by Mark Kelley

73

making it a federal offense to harm or harass any marine mammal in U.S. waters. The amended act in 1986 specifically outlawed shooting orcas. The greatest threat to the orcas today is the declining number of wild salmon and mammals on which they prey.

Most orcas killed by humans today die by accident, as the bycatch of commercial fisheries. Orcas can drown if they become tangled in fishing nets or are scooped up by bottom-dragging trawlers.

Orcas haven't always been seen as competitors to fishermen or a commercial catch for whalers. There are tales of orcas helping seafarers hunt whales in return for the whale's tongue (the orcas' favorite part), and even of orcas herding fish for fishermen — like sheep dogs with fins.

The orcas' popularity has presented another problem for them. More than 150 orcas were taken alive from U.S. and Canadian waters and put on display. The orca captures began in 1962. Trainers liked working with captive orcas because the animals are so intelligent and trainable. In aquariums, some orcas quickly learned not to fear humans. Some even bred successfully in captivity. However, many died within a few years of capture. Many fell silent living alone or sharing a small tank with another orca that didn't speak the same language. Cut off from social bonds, a captive orca may become depressed or aggressive. Sometimes, its dorsal fin would collapse. This is rarely seen in the wild and thought to be a sign of stress or poor health. Some pods that had several reproductive females taken have not recovered and are currently in decline. Despite the enjoyment of seeing orcas in aquariums, public opinion in the United States turned against capturing orcas for public display. The practice was outlawed by 1977.

Keeping our oceans and waterways clean will ensure that Alaska continues to be one of the best places to see healthy orcas in the wild.

photo by Mark Kelley

Killer whale facts

		Average	Range
Length	Female		23-28 feet
	Male		26-33 feet
	At birth	8 feet	7-8 feet
Weight	Female	4 tons	4-7 tons
	Male	8 tons	8-11 tons
	At birth	400 pounds	
Dorsal fin	Male	6 feet	
	Female	3 feet	
Behaviors	Blow		Up to 10 feet
	Dive: time	4-10 minutes	1-20 minutes
	Dive: depth	Feeding dives under 800 feet	
	Speed	3-7 miles per hour	
	Adult feeding habits	4% of body weight per day	
Lifespan	Female	50 years	50-70 years
	Male	30 years	30-50 years
Sexual Maturity	Female	15 years	12-14 years
	Male	12-14 years	10-15 years
Birthing	Gestation	17 months	
	Lactation	Over 12 months	6-10 months
Populations	World	Unknown	
	Alaska	1,500 whales	
Pod Range	Resident	250 mile radius	250-1,000 miles
	Transient	900 mile radius	900-1,500 miles

PHOTOGRAPHERS

Photo by Mone Poulsen

MARK KELLEY has photographed Southeast Alaska for the past 25 years. His photos have appeared in hundreds of publications and on the covers of over 200 publications. He has six photo books to his credit, and *Alaska's Watchable Whales* marks the second book that he has shared the photo credits with another photographer. In addition to books and magazines, he publishes two annual calendars and an extensive line of note cards. He lives in Juneau with his wife, Jan, and their two sons, Gabe and Owen.

JOHN HYDE
My goal as a photographer is to create images that inspire. Over the years my work has enabled me to explore many of Southeast Alaska's wild places and spend time with the wild animals that live here. Whales are particularly intriguing. Not knowing where or when they will next appear adds to their mystery. What exactly goes on when they are below the surface? What goes through the minds of these creatures with brains equal to our own? We can conjecture, but no one really knows. The questions go on and on and that is what draws me to them.

I make Southeast Alaska my home because I find its raw beauty especially attractive.

The opportunity to share some of my experiences with others through photography brings me great satisfaction and keeps me looking forward to future opportunities.

TECHNICAL NOTES: All the photos in this book were taken on the wild whale waters of Southeast Alaska, and none were digitally enhanced or manipulated. Mark Kelley shot all his photos with Nikon cameras and lens using 35mm Fuji Velvia slide film. The lens used for his images ranged from 20mm to his 400mm. John Hyde shot his images with Canon gear using mostly 35mm Fuji slide film.

photo by Mark Kelley

ACKNOWLEDGMENTS
by MARK KELLEY

photo by Mark Kelley

My goal was to publish a beautiful photo book with the most accurate and up-to-date whale information available. To that end, I thank Dean Matkin and Jan Straley for reading and commenting on the text. They are both recognized marine biologists and Southeast Alaska whale specialists. Through their efforts, the book is as accurate as possible. Any misstatements or inaccuracies are the fault of the publisher.

Many of my photos in this book would not have been possible without the unwavering support from conception to completion of Jim Collins from Allen Marine. I thank him for his friendship, support and our many whale scouting trips. Even if the whale shows were not good, we had a good time.

I thank my good friend, Larry Persily, who endlessly and selflessly helps me edit all the copy on all my projects.

John Hyde is one of best and most dedicated wildlife photographers in Alaska. I thank him for allowing me to publish a small portion of his incredible whale portfolio.

Once again, I thank Laura Lucas for pulling all the pieces of the puzzle together and designing such a beautiful book.

I thank Linda Daniel, Scott Foster and Lynn Schooler whom all agreed to lend their writing talents to this project.

I thank my summer worker, Lena Darnall, for researching the whale literature and giving this project a baseline of whale facts and figures.

I thank Paul Johnson and Tami Mulick from Gull Cove Lodge for letting me hang out at their lodge while searching for whales.

The whale researchers of the world have my thanks. All the information in this book came from their work published in books, papers, lectures and websites. To that end, I plan to take a small portion of the sale of each book and give it back to the whale research community in the form of an annual grant.

Finally, I thank my wife, Jan, and our sons, Gabe and Owen, for supporting me through all my projects and for making it all worthwhile.

following page photo by Mark Kelley